Everyday Life

Liz Gogerly

W

FRANKLIN WATTS

LONDON • SYDNEY

Designer Jason Billin
Editor Sarah Ridley
Art Director Jonathan Hair
Editor-in-Chief John C. Miles
Picture research Diana Morris

First published in 2006 by Franklin Watts

Copyright © 2006 Franklin Watts

Franklin Watts
338 Euston Road
London NW1 3BH

Franklin Watts Australia
Hachette Children's Books
Level 17/207 Kent Street
Sydney NSW 2000

A CIP catalogue record for this book
is available from the British Library.

Dewey classification number: 942.05

ISBN: 978 0 7496 6450 3

Printed in China

Picture credits

Adams Picture Library/Alamy: 6
Bibliothèque Nationale, Paris/Bridgeman Art Library: 13
T Alena Brett: 4, 25
British Library, London/Bridgeman Art Library: 11
British Museum, London/HIP/Topfoto: 12
Burghley House,Stamford/ Mark Fiennes/Bridgeman Art Library: 9
Mary Evans Picture Library: 17
Geoffrey Frosh/NTPL: 19
Hatfield House, Hertfordshire/Bridgeman Art Library: cover, 1, 15
David Levenson/NTPL: 20
Longleat House, Wiltshire/Bridgeman Art Library: 14
Musée des Beaux-Arts, Lille/Bridgeman Art Library: 18
The Museum of London: 24
Museum of London/Bridgeman Art Library: 21
Private Collection/Bridgeman Art Library: 8, 10, 22, 23, 26, 29
Private Collection/© Philip Mould, Historical Portraits Ltd, London/Bridgeman Art Library: 5
Ben Ramos/Alamy: 16
Society of Antiquaries/Bridgeman Art Library: 3, 7
V&A Images: 28
Woodmansterne/Topfoto: 27

Every attempt has been made to clear copyright. Should there be any inadvertent omission please apply to the publisher for rectification.

Note to parents and teachers:
Every effort has been made by the Publishers to ensure that the websites in this book are suitable for children, that they are of the highest educational value, and that they contain no inappropriate or offensive material. However, because of the nature of the Internet, it is impossible to guarantee that the contents of these sites will not be altered. We strongly advise that Internet access is supervised by a responsible adult.

Contents

Monarchs of the Tudor age

In 1485 Henry Tudor, Earl of Richmond, defeated Richard III at the Battle of Bosworth. This marked the end of the Wars of the Roses, a conflict that had raged for nearly 50 years. Henry Tudor was crowned King Henry VII and the Tudor age began.

Henry VII (reigned 1485-1509) inherited a country weakened by years of war. During his peaceful reign he spent the country's money carefully and ruled well. Henry VII died in 1509 and was succeeded by his second son, Henry.

Henry VIII

Henry VIII (1509-1547)
As a young man, Henry VIII was popular but later he brought religious unrest to England by splitting the Church of England from the Roman Catholic Church. Henry liked to live well and he also spent a lot of money on his army and navy. He became desperate to father a male heir and married six times. Henry divorced his wives Catherine of Aragon and Anne of Cleves. He had Anne Boleyn and Catherine Howard executed. Jane Seymour died after childbirth. Henry died in 1547, and the crown passed to his only son Edward.

Edward VI (1547-1553)

Henry's son Edward VI was just nine years old when he took the throne. However, he was clever and people had high hopes for their new tudor king. Sadly, Edward died at the age of 16 and was succeeded by Mary, Henry VIII's daughter by Catherine of Aragon.

Mary I (1553-1558) and Elizabeth I (1558-1603)

A devout Roman Catholic, Mary I was never very popular with her people. She died in 1558 and her sister, Elizabeth, who was the daughter of Henry VIII and Anne Boleyn, was crowned queen. Elizabeth went on to become one of the most beloved monarchs of all time. Elizabeth never married or had children, so she was the last Tudor to sit on the English throne. She died in 1603 and her cousin, James VI of Scotland, a Stuart, succeeded her.

Queen Elizabeth I

 Tudor society

There was a strict social structure in Tudor times, where almost everyone had a "master". At the top was the monarch, whose only master was God. Nobles, knights and gentlemen were next. Below them came merchants and businessmen, then craftsmen and farmers. Next were servants and labourers, whose lives were controlled by the people who paid them. At the bottom there were the homeless unemployed who answered to no one and who were viewed as a threat to society.

The growth of towns

At the beginning of the Tudor age England had a population of less than four million people. By the time Elizabeth I died, the population had grown to about six million.

Throughout this time there was a steady stream of people moving from the countryside to the cities and towns. Often they were in search of work as there were less jobs in farming. The towns, being centres of trade, provided jobs for merchants and market workers. There was also work for skilled tradesmen and craftsmen. Many towns doubled in size during Tudor times. London grew from a population of about 60,000 in 1520 to over 200,000 in 1600.

Urban life

Life in cities and towns could be hard and dangerous, especially for the poor. Houses were built close together and were overcrowded. People often worked and lived in the same place. They had workshops in their homes, and shops spilled out from the front of houses. The busy streets became dirty and there was no proper drainage. People poured their waste out of the window or into cesspits. The smell was appalling and diseases spread quickly. Thousands died when bubonic plague struck.

These Tudor houses in Lavenham, Suffolk, were built by families who had grown rich through the wool trade that flourished locally.

Wealthy families

Wealthy people often built their homes on the edge of the city, close to open spaces and fresh air. If disease struck, they could usually escape to a second home in the countryside. In towns, successful families built fine new homes in the centre.

At the heart of the action

Cities were exciting places to be. London was the centre of government and the ruling monarch spent many months living there. There were splendid weddings and royal parades to watch, as well as theatres, taverns and inns to visit and markets and fairs for shopping and trading.

An Italian's view

"All the streets are so badly paved that they get wet at the slightest quantity of water... Then a vast amount of evil-smelling mud is formed, which does not disappear quickly but lasts a long time, in fact nearly the whole year round. The citizens, therefore, in order to remove this mud and filth from their boots, are accustomed to spread fresh rushes on the floors of all houses..."

Andreas Franciscus, an Italian visiting London in 1497.

This view of London shows part of Edward VI's coronation procession from the Tower of London (far left) to Westminster in 1547. Old St Paul's Cathedral is the building with the spire (far right). London was described as the most magnificent city in Europe.

Life in the countryside

Towns and cities were growing but most people still lived in the countryside. Ordinary people often lived their entire lives in the same village.

Most villages were close-knit communities. People helped each other and shared tools. The land in the countryside was usually owned by the nobility or gentlemen. They paid farm labourers for each day's work, or gave them food and housing in exchange for their labour. Sometimes farmers managed to buy their own land but usually they had to lease their fields from wealthy landowners.

A hard life

Most villagers grew all their food themselves in the fields surrounding the village and in their garden plots. They lived in small houses, mostly made of wood. The landlord did not always keep them in good order.

The whole family usually crammed into one dark room, with a fire in the centre. As many houses didn't have a proper chimney, they were filled with smoke. There was hardly any furniture and people slept on straw-filled mattresses. It must have been difficult to sleep, store food, cook, clean clothes and wash in such a small space.

Tudor village houses were often made of wood. Only chimneys, if people had them, were made of brick or stone.

The privileged few

Life was very different for rich landowners. Many built grand houses on their country estates. These had huge kitchens packed full of servants preparing luxurious foods. Most rooms had a fireplace with a chimney. By modern standards they didn't have much furniture but they did have tables, stools, cupboards and four-poster beds. Some Tudor farmers and merchants grew rich enough to build themselves fine homes.

Built between 1555 and 1587, Burghley House in Lincolnshire is one of the largest and grandest houses of the Tudor era.

Getting around

The countryside in Tudor times wasn't as cut off as you might think. There was a network of roads, known as the King's Highway, that linked the major towns. These roads were used for going to and from market by people who were buying or selling the produce grown in the country. Horses were very expensive so poor people walked great distances.

Working in the countryside

In the countryside farming was the main way of making a living. Most people worked as farm labourers for the local landowner, or lord.

Being a farm labourer was hard work and the day began at sunrise. At harvest time the fields were filled with people cutting the crop with sickles. In the following months, people ploughed the fields with the help of horses or oxen, and sowed seeds and planted crops by hand.

The sheep arrive

During Tudor times there was a crisis in farming. Farm labourers began asking for higher wages which many farmers could not afford to pay. At the same time, the wool industry became very profitable. So, from 1450 onwards, in some areas of the country, farmers and rich landowners started to turn their fields over to grazing land for sheep. Walls were built to keep animals in and land once used to graze the animals of poorer people was no longer available. Compared with growing crops, not nearly as many labourers were needed. Many farm labourers struggled to survive.

A 16th-century woodcut illustration showing farm labourers ploughing with oxen.

Weavers and craftsmen

The rise of the wool industry did bring some extra work to the countryside. More people learnt how to spin and weave wool into cloth. They did this at home, which is where the term "cottage industry" comes from. Though men were considered to be the main income earner in a family, these were jobs that women could do too.

There was always a need for skilled craftsmen to prepare and make leather goods such as shoes, or saddles for horses. There was also plenty of work for blacksmiths who made iron goods, such as farm tools and horse shoes.

Shepherding was a traditional job in the countryside. These shepherds are shearing their sheep.

Weather talk

The Tudors were just as fascinated by the weather as we are today. Many of them commented on it in their diaries and letters. A freezing cold Christmas of 1536 led to the River Thames being frozen over. The summer of 1540 was so hot that all the ponds dried up. Today, much of our food can be imported from abroad but back in Tudor times, a poor harvest due to bad weather meant that people died of hunger.

Making a living

During Tudor times, many people grew wealthy by selling goods to other countries. English ports grew in size as they became centres of the trade in English cloth, coal, tin, iron, sugar and glass.

The craftsmen who made the goods to sell, like the spinners, weavers and dyers of the wool industry, joined groups called guilds. Guilds had rules about how people should be trained and set a standard for their work. Young boys who hoped to become skilled craftsmen or tradesmen became apprentices. This meant they lived and worked with an employer for seven years while they learned. The guild also helped its members if they were ill and weren't able to work.

Apprentices at work in a Tudor goldsmith's workshop.

Go and visit

The Guildhall in Lavenham, Suffolk, was built by one of the guilds that regulated the wool trade in the town. It is a good example of the headquarters of a Tudor guild, and is open during the summer months.

12

Tudor industries

Ship-building became more important as merchants needed ships to transport their goods abroad. Coal mines opened up in the north of England. The coal was sold abroad and used to fuel fires in the sugar refining, glass-making and soap-boiling trades. There was also plenty of work for skilled tradesmen, such as carpenters or stonemasons, as people built new homes or warehouses.

A rise in literacy

The number of people who could read and write grew during Tudor times, although most women could not do either. Many boys were taught in the new grammar schools (see pages 16-17). Often they became clerks, bankers, priests or teachers. Some of them went into another booming trade – printing and bookselling. People who went to university could find jobs as doctors or lawyers.

Increased literacy meant that more books were printed, and there was a great demand for paper. This picture shows paper-making.

 "Masterless men"

Not everybody had a job in Tudor England and some people had to beg to survive. These jobless people were called "vagrants" or "vagabonds". With no master to answer to, they were viewed as a threat to society. The number of homeless people rose steeply during Tudor times because there was less farm work available (see page 10). Various laws were brought in to control them and to make begging illegal.

The Tudor family

Family life was important to the Tudors. A man was firmly at the head of the family, as this Tudor book about family life states: "For as a body can have but one head, so a household, if it is to prosper, can have but one lord and master."

Portrait of Lord Cobham and his family. Wealthy families had many children, often as many as 12.

People from wealthy families usually married early, maybe as early as 12 for a girl, or 14 for a boy. Often their parents decided who they would marry. This was because property and money were involved and families felt it was important that they married into a family like their own.

Ordinary families

People from ordinary families had more freedom about who they married. They usually worked until their mid-twenties, as farmers, servants or apprentices. Young men often waited until they learned a trade before they got married. Only then did they have enough money to set up their own home.

A skimmington ride

Husbands who were bossed about by their wives upset what the Tudors saw as the natural order of things in the same way as "masterless men" (see page 13) did. As a punishment, some villages organised a skimmington ride for the man in question, parading him through the streets while people jeered at him and played loud music.

Tudor women

Women were described as the daughter or wife of somebody. Property usually belonged to men and was passed down to other males in the family. Even though women were considered less powerful than men they had an important part to play in family life. They were in charge of running the household and looked after the children and servants. Many poorer women had other work too. They might help on the land or they worked at home doing jobs such as spinning and weaving wool.

This famous picture shows a Tudor wedding at Bermondsey, near London.

Children at school and play

In Tudor times children were raised to know their place. Parents were stricter than today and regularly beat or punished their children.

Very poor children were expected to work or help in the house as soon as they were old enough. Many parents sent their children to live with other families, in order to learn craft or trade skills (an apprenticeship) or, in the case of wealthy children, to learn good manners.

Girls

Girls from all backgrounds did not go to school. People tended to believe that the most important lesson that a girl could learn was how to be a good wife. This meant being obedient and learning how to run a house, cook, sew and grow vegetables. Only a few girls from wealthy families had tutors to teach them to read and write.

 Go and visit

Henry VIII opened the first grammar schools in England. Known as the King's Schools, these provided an education for boys over the age of seven. Many more grammars were founded during the reign of Edward VI and Elizabeth I.
The Edward VI Grammar School in Stratford-upon-Avon has one room that has been a classroom since Tudor times. The playwright William Shakespeare was a pupil and once sat at its desks.

Boys

Education for wealthy boys began at home with a tutor. Later they were sent away to boarding school, paid for by their parents. Some boys from less well-off families still had an education. From the age of four they went to church schools. When they reached seven they attended grammar school, which was free if they won a scholarship.

Toys and games

Tudor children knew how to have fun, when they had time. Country children played outside and climbed trees. Children from wealthier families learned to ride horses, hunt, play musical instruments and dance. Poorer children played with homemade wooden toys, like spinning tops, while wealthier ones might have a rocking horse or a doll. Inflated pig's bladders made good footballs, while pebbles were used to play marbles. Team games were popular too. Children could play at fighting on horseback, blindman's buff or leapfrog.

The school day

School children spent most of their time learning Latin. They learnt huge amounts by heart. The day was very long, lasting from 6 am until 5.30 pm, six days a week.

A painting of a Tudor schoolroom

"Our daily bread"

Those Tudors who could afford to enjoyed three meals a day. But many people managed with less.

Soon after waking at 5 or 6 am people took breakfast. Then at about 11 am they ate the main meal of the day, which was dinner. The evening meal took place when the working day had ended and was called supper. Bread was the main food for everybody and in England most people ate about 450g of bread each day.

This 16th-century religious picture, although showing an incident in the Bible, actually gives a good idea of what a Tudor kitchen looked like. Meat was roasted on spits in front of the fire.

Meat and few veg

The diet of ordinary people living in England was slightly better than that of other ordinary Europeans. As well as bread, English people ate a lot of meat, poultry, fish and dairy products. Wealthy people ate few vegetables, although poorer families ate them in stews or in a kind of soup called a pottage. People ate what was in season as most food did not keep. Some new types of fruit and vegetables were arriving from the "New World" (the Americas), such as tomatoes and potatoes. Only the rich could afford to buy them.

Banquets

Rich people had a reputation for eating too much. At the court of Henry VIII it wasn't unusual to have banquets with ten different courses. Foods like venison or even roast swan were eaten. In 1541 a new law tried to stop people eating too much. The law stated that nobles were allowed a maximum of seven dishes at a meal, gentlemen could eat five dishes and everyone else could have just four dishes.

A large fire would have warmed diners as they ate in the hall of Sutton House in London. Exotic carpets from the Middle East were an expensive luxury. They were used to cover tables.

Sweet foods

The Tudors liked their food sweet and honey was used in many meat dishes, as well as in biscuits and pies. Wealthy people could afford sugar, a luxury from the New World. Many people began to pay for their love of sugar with rotten teeth.

 Go and visit

Hampton Court Palace in London is one of many large houses around the country where you can see what the kitchens of wealthy Tudors looked like.

Clothes and fashion

In Tudor times clothes were a display of a person's position in society. Clothing was so important that in 1510 parliament passed a law stating what everybody should wear. If anybody disobeyed this law they could be fined or punished.

Only the royal family could wear gold cloth or anything purple. Servants, labourers and farmers were not allowed to use material that cost over a given amount. Nor were they allowed to wear gold rings.

Ordinary clothing

Most people were pleased to have clothing that kept them warm and often only owned one set of clothes, homemade from linen or wool and often blue or brown. They also wore linen underclothes, which prevented their outer clothes from getting too sweaty.

It was easy to tell someone's job by the clothes they wore. Working women wore long dresses of plain cloth over woollen stockings. Labourers wore a loose wool tunic over breeches (long shorts) and stockings. Somebody higher up in society who didn't work in the fields, like a merchant or a clerk, wore a long gown. Children were dressed as mini-adults.

Tudor clothes for ordinary people were often made from a coarse brown woollen fabric.

Go and visit

The Victoria and Albert Museum in London has a huge collection of historical clothes. Alternatively, look out for Tudor re-enactments in your local area, such as those at Kentwell Hall in Suffolk. There you will be able to see people of all ages dressed in the clothes of a particular period in history.

Fashion for the wealthy

Fashions came and went throughout the Tudor age but the dress for wealthy people was always rich and extravagant. Men and women's clothes were embroidered with emblems such as flowers. Henry VIII impressed foreign visitors with masses of jewels sewn on his clothes. His appearance made them believe England was a rich nation. Elizabeth I also dressed to impress. Her dresses were covered in dazzling embroidery.

Clothes for the wealthy were made from rich fabrics and beautifully embroidered, like these examples.

Go and visit

Hall i' th' Wood is a museum based in a Tudor house in Bolton, Greater Manchester. It hosts events where you can dress up in Tudor costume and experience 16th-century life.

Pale is beautiful

It was fashionable for the wealthy classes to be pale skinned. This was because it showed you were rich enough not to have to labour outdoors. Women used potions of white roses and water lilies to help them keep their skins as white as possible. Some women used a face powder made from white lead – they did not realise that it was poisonous. Nobody washed very much so perfumes were a must. Many people splashed perfume on their gloves and wafted them under their noses.

Health and medicine

Most Tudors were dead before they reached the age of 50. In Europe, as many as one in five children died within their first year of life.

The average number of years a person was expected to live was 32 for a man and 35 for a woman. But, if you were poor and lived in the city the chances were you would die in your twenties. The reason so many people died was because nobody understood how diseases were spread. Nor did they have the medicine or health care to help them get well.

The link with dirt

One of the biggest problems was hygiene. Diseases like dysentery, called "the flux", were passed through drinking dirty water. With no system in place to keep drinking water separate from sewage, this was a common illness. People rarely washed or took baths. This made it easy for diseases like typhus to spread as it passed from one person to the next by body lice. Bubonic plague was spread by the fleas of the rats that were common around people's homes.

Surviving the agony of a leg amputation without anaesthetic was just the beginning for this patient, in an age before antibiotics.

The "royal touch"

One illness was treated not by doctors or wise women, but by the monarch. This was scrofula - tuberculosis of the lymph nodes in the neck. People believed that the king or queen had special powers to cure this unpleasant disease because of their link with God. Religious services where sufferers experienced the "royal touch" were common. In the picture on the right, Mary I is shown touching a sufferer, while a priest reads the service. The last monarch to "touch" was Queen Anne, in the early 1700s.

Tudor doctors

If you were ill in Tudor times then you could visit a physician, a surgeon or an apothecary. If you were poor you usually saw a wise woman (see panel). She was also called upon to help at childbirth. Physicians were the best-educated medical people but they relied heavily on blood-letting, either cutting the patient to let a lot of blood flow into a cup, or using a leech to suck the blood. Surgeons could set broken bones and amputate limbs, which they did without anaesthetic. Apothecaries sold herbal cures. All too often "the cure" made a person even more ill.

Wise women

Generations of wise women treated ill people, using cures passed down by word of mouth from their mothers or grandmothers. Often the cure involved herbs, some of which were probably quite helpful. A typical cure for a cold was made from blackberries. Other "cures" included using the cut-up body of a mouse to treat warts or toothache. Mashed mole was supposed to be a cure for baldness!

Ways of worship

The Tudors were much more religious than we are today. Most people believed in God and hoped to go to heaven when they died.

People also believed that they should obey the monarch, as this was God's will. When Henry VIII became King of England he was a practising Roman Catholic. This meant he worshipped God with church services held in Latin and followed the teachings of the Pope in Rome. His people were expected to follow his example, even though most of them couldn't understand a word of what was being said.

A set of 16th-century sacred vessels (with their case) for the Roman Catholic Mass – a bottle for wine, a chalice (cup) and a paten (communion plate).

The Reformation

During the 16th century there was a movement in Europe called the Reformation. People began to argue about the right way to worship God and to question the power of the Roman Catholic Church. They set up Protestant churches but, in Catholic England, Protestant preachers could be burned to death.

The break with Rome

In 1532 Henry VIII wanted to divorce his first wife, Catherine of Aragon, and marry his pregnant lover, Anne Boleyn. He hoped she would give birth to a male heir to succeed him. The Pope, the head of the Roman Catholic Church, refused Henry a divorce so, in fury, Henry broke away, declaring himself the Head of the Church of England and granting his own divorce. England was swept into religious unrest.

Dying for their faith

Henry's daughter Mary I was a devout Roman Catholic. During her short reign, she had hundreds of Protestants burned for refusing to return to the Roman Catholic faith. Her sister, Elizabeth I, was a Protestant but tried to follow a "middle way" in matters of religion. The religious situation did improve but Catholic plots against Elizabeth towards the end of her reign meant that Catholics were persecuted.

An English Bible

William Tyndale was a preacher who translated the Bible from its original Greek and Hebrew into English. He wanted everyone to be able to read the Bible for themselves. However, the Church felt threatened by this idea and Tyndale had to leave England to finish his work in Europe. Copies of his Bible were smuggled back into England but were banned by Henry VIII in 1530. When Henry broke away from the Roman Catholic Church, he made a complete turnaround and ordered that there should be a copy of Tyndale's English Bible in every church in England.

Mary I (1553-1558) ordered the execution of hundreds of Protestants.

Crime and punishment

" It was so loathsomely and filthily kept that it was not fit for any man to come into... "

A visitor to Bridewell Prison in London in 1598 made these comments. He might have been talking about any jail for common criminals in Tudor times. Dungeons were dark with heavy doors and small barred windows. Prisoners were sometimes placed in flooded cells or were eaten alive by hungry rats. Beyond were rooms with foul equipment used for torture, of which the rack was the most feared. The prisoner's legs and arms were tied to winches set in a wooden frame; these were turned until the ropes were tight and the prisoner's joints popped out of their sockets.

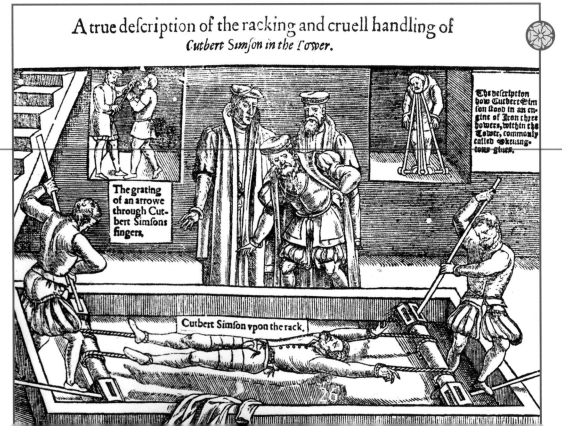

A true description of the racking and cruell handling of *Cutbert Simson in the Tower.*

The grating of an arrowe through Cutbert Simsons fingers,

The description how Cutbert Simson stood in an engine of Iron three howers, within the Tower, commonly called Skeuingtons gliues,

Cutbert Simson vpon the rack.

Cuthbert Simson was tortured in several ways, including the rack, for being a follower of the Protestant faith during the reign of Mary I.

Wealthy prisoners

As with most aspects of life in Tudor times, it was different if you were rich or royalty. You might be sent to a better prison such as the Tower of London. Some rooms were more comfortable but the methods of torture were just as unpleasant.

The stocks and other punishments

Petty criminals or thieves were usually whipped or placed in the stocks, rather than being sent to prison. Members of the public pelted the criminal in the stocks with rotten food. Some criminals had a limb chopped off or they had an ear nailed to the stocks. A law passed in 1572 ordered that vagrants (homeless beggars) be punished by being whipped, or branded (burnt) on the ear. The death sentence was common in Tudor times too, sometimes for minor crimes, but also for murder and theft, heresy and treason. All of these punishments became public events watched by everyone.

Being put in the village stocks - which pinned the offender's legs - was a shaming punishment.

Having fun in Tudor times

The wealthier you were, the more time you had to have fun. But for both rich and poor, there were plenty of public holidays, such as May Day and church festival days, when everyone had time to dance, eat, drink, play sport or watch plays.

Sports such as hunting, falconry, jousting, tennis and bowls were pastimes for the wealthy. Henry VII and Henry VIII both enjoyed a game of tennis, though the game was quite different to "modern" tennis. The rich also played indoor games like cards, chess, draughts and dice. Henry VIII loved to gamble when he played cards. Music and theatre were also important (see page 29), as well as dancing. News of complicated dances created at the Royal Court spread to wealthy people living in the countryside.

This Tudor embroidered scene shows nobles hunting.

Ale house, tavern and inn

In Tudor times taverns and ale houses became popular. Taverns were slightly more respectable than ale houses. The ale house served only beer or ale while taverns offered food and wine. Taverns and ale houses were well known for being noisy, drunken places where fights easily broke out. English inns sold food and drink but they also offered rooms for the night and stables for horses. This was important in an age when it could take days to get anywhere.

Fun for the poor

Poor people worked hard but they also knew how to enjoy themselves. Public holidays were times to dance, eat and drink too much. People also joined in sports such as archery. Henry VIII needed archers in times of war so it became law for men between 17 and 60 to keep a longbow and four arrows. Village competitions tested people's archery skills.

Football in Tudor times was a violent game with few rules. The ball was thrown or kicked and the goalposts could be miles apart. The Tudors also liked watching cruel sports. Cock-fighting – in which two cockerels fought to the death – was popular with everyone.

Plays and the theatre

In towns and villages people flocked to see plays and pageants performed by travelling actors. The plot was often based on a Bible story or a story from ancient Greece or Rome. In the cities, the theatre became more popular during Tudor times, partly because Elizabeth I enjoyed watching plays.

The first purpose-built London theatre was called "The Theatre" and was built in 1576. Next came the Rose and the Swan theatres. The famous Globe theatre was built in 1599. Some Tudor plays, such as those written by William Shakespeare and Christopher Marlowe, are still performed today.

GLOSSARY

amputate
To cut off something, e.g a part of the body.

apprentice
A person who learns a trade by being employed in it for an agreed period of time at a low wage.

archery
Shooting with a bow and arrow.

banquet
A meal for a large number of people to celebrate a special occasion.

cesspits
A hole or pit where human waste is thrown.

clerk
A person employed in an office, bank or shop, to keep records and accounts.

cock-fighting
A cruel blood sport where two cockerels fight each other to the death. People place bets on which cockerel they think will win the fight.

dysentery
A disease of the intestines that causes severe, bloody diarrhoea.

grammar schools
Schools that were originally founded in the sixteenth century to teach Latin grammar.

heir
Someone who will be given money, property or a title when somebody else dies.

heresy
A belief or practice that is different to what is normally accepted.

jerkin
A short sleeveless jacket.

jousting
A contest between two knights, riding horses and carrying lances. Each knight tries to knock the other off his horse.

holy day
A religious festival.

lease
To enter an agreement with a landowner to use his land for a certain amount of time.

mass
A Roman Catholic church service.

merchant
Somebody who sells goods for profit. Often they trade with other countries.

ornate
Highly decorated.

plague
A deadly disease that spreads quickly over a large area. It usually refers to bubonic plague, which was common in Tudor times.

plough
A tool that cuts furrows into farmland to allow seeds to be planted.

Protestants
Christians who rejected the authority of the Roman Catholic Church and the Pope in Rome and instead focused on scripture as the best way to worship God.

revised
Changed and updated.

Roman Catholic
Christians who believe that the Pope in Rome is the head of their religion.

sickle
A handle with a sharp blade used to cut stalks of corn.

stocks
A device to punish people by trapping their legs so that they cannot move.

stonemasons
People who are skilled in cutting and using stone.

succeeded
To have taken over a position from somebody else.

tanning
Taking the raw hide of an animal and treating it with chemicals or salts to make it into leather.

treason
The crime of betraying your country or plotting against the King or Queen.

TIMELINE

22 August 1485 Henry becomes King Henry VII.

28 June 1491 Henry Tudor is born to King Henry VII and Elizabeth of York.

21 April 1509 Henry Tudor becomes King Henry VIII of England.

25 January 1533 King Henry VIII marries Anne Boleyn.

7 September 1533 Elizabeth Tudor is born to King Henry VIII and Anne Boleyn.

17 November 1534 The Act of Supremacy is passed by Parliament; it declares the English monarch to be the Supreme Head of the Church of England.

18 March 1536 Dissolution of the monasteries begins.

19 May 1536 King Henry VIII's second wife, Anne Boleyn, is executed.

12 October 1537 King Henry VIII's only son, Prince Edward, is born.

13 February 1542 King Henry VIII's fifth wife, Catherine Howard, is executed.

28 January 1547 Edward Tudor becomes King Edward VI.

6 July 1553 King Edward VI dies.

3 August 1553 Mary Tudor becomes Queen Mary I.

25 July 1554 Queen Mary I marries King Philip II of Spain.

17 November 1558 Elizabeth Tudor becomes Queen Elizabeth I.

29 April 1559 The Elizabethan religious settlement is passed by Parliament.

19 June 1566 King James VI of Scotland, son of Mary Queen of Scots, is born.

24 July 1567 Mary, Queen of Scots abdicates her throne.

8 February 1587 Mary, Queen of Scots is executed at Fotheringhay Castle.

31 July 1588 Defeat of the Spanish Armada.

24 March 1603 Queen Elizabeth I dies; King James VI of Scotland becomes king of England.

PLACES TO VISIT

Burghley House, Stamford, Lincolnshire
Experience the magnificence of a Tudor country house.

The Globe Theatre, Bankside, London
Visit the reconstructed Shakespeare's Globe Theatre to see new productions of Shakespeare's plays.

The Edward VI Grammar School, Stratford-upon-Avon, Warwickshire – You can make an appointment to visit this fascinating school which included Shakespeare as a pupil.
http://www.kingedwardvi.warwickshire.sch.uk/

Hampton Court Palace, East Molesey, Surrey
Visit the State Apartments of Henry VIII and the enormous Tudor kitchens.

The Geffrye Museum, Kingsland Road, London – What did a Tudor room look like? Find out at this museum where furniture, textiles, paintings and objects are displayed.

Kentwell Hall, Long Melford, Suffolk
A Tudor stately home restored to much of its former glory, the scene for re-enactments of life in Tudor times.

WEBSITES

http://www.tudorbritain.org/
A fabulous site for children learning about the Tudors created by the Victoria and Albert Museum.

http://www.geffrye-museum.org.uk/kidszone/garden/
Have fun designing your own Elizabethan garden.

http://www.museumoflondon.org.uk/targetthetudors/
Learn more about everyday life in Tudor times when you visit this lively and entertaining site.

http://www.maryrose.org/explore/menu.htm
http://www.gtj.org.uk/trails/tudor/index.html
Get some hands-on experience of the Tudor age when you join the crew of the Tudor warship the *Mary Rose*.

INDEX